Amounting
to
Nothing
POEMS

Paul Quenon, OCSO

PARACLETE PRESS
BREWSTER, MASSACHUSETTS

2019 First Printing

Amounting to Nothing: Poems

Copyright © 2019 by The Abbey of Gethsemani

ISBN 978-1-64060-201-4

The Paraclete Press name and logo (dove on cross) are trademarks of Paraclete Press, Inc.

Library of Congress Cataloging-in-Publication Data

Names: Quenon, Paul, author.
Title: Amounting to nothing : poems / Paul Quenon.
Description: Brewster, MA : Paraclete Press, Inc., 2019.
Identifiers: LCCN 2019002146 | ISBN 9781640602014 (tradepaper)
Classification: LCC PR9199.3.Q45 A6 2019 | DDC 811/.54—dc23
LC record available at https://lccn.loc.gov/2019002146

10 9 8 7 6 5 4 3 2 1

Published by Paraclete Press
Brewster, Massachusetts
www.paracletepress.com

Printed in the United States of America

I Getting Nowhere

II Busy at Non-Doing

III A Community of Creatures

IV Ritual Instinct

As long as the soul is anywhere,
she is not in the greatest of God,
which is nowhere.
  —*Meister Eckhart, Sermon 39*

PARACLETE **POETRY** *Series Editor*
Mark S. Burrows

I

Getting Nowhere

Mad Monk's Life Ambition

Sorry monk that I am,
I never amounted to nothing.

Did someone lay on a jinx and say:
You'll never amount to nothing?

How sad, since I took nothing
as my monastic goal.

I still don't amount to nothing,
still think I'm something.

I hardly amount to a hill of beans but
this already is too much of something.

What ever might you mount
to amount to nothing?

Where is that magical mountain?
where that weird agility to climb a hill of humus,

humility so grounded it ascends by descending?
a humility that does not know it is a virtue.

When I find it, if I ever do,
comparing something with nothing will cease.

Any measure or judgment of my own
itself amounts to nothing.

Thin Host

Such a flake of a thing—
this thin wafer!

Hardly the highest achievement
of human nature,
culture or imagination.

Who could love it?
Such humility as this—

simply divine,
humanly simple,
pressed out and baked
to be

the hidden heartbeat of the Cosmic Christ,
the center of all reality.

Undefined

The closer I get to the bell tower
the louder it says

Definitely
Definitely

but leaves out definitely what.

What is my life
but an undefined definitely

occupying space and time
in the vastness of

the - - - - - - - - -

God

A soft, round word
        Mother taught me

said putting my mouth
        in a circle

with soft G way back in my
        deep swallow cave

followed by silent D
        front tongue closing

cloud scarcely seen
        then gone

a quiet word

told in a quiet
        moment

when first I learned
        to shape the word

        God.

Watchman

Watchman, what of the night?

What of it?

What do you watch?

Nothing.

What then of nothing?

Can't say. Seems something
always gets in the way.

Something like what?

Fireflies, whippoorwills, rain smells.

Of course! What else did you expect?

Nothing.

Then why watch?

Haven't found nothing yet.

Why not?

I expected it.

Expected what?

Nothing.

That sounds so easy!

Too easy for me. Been trying too hard.

At what?

Just to do it. Watching. Without doing anything.

Alone with the Alone

I just want to go hide.
They'll all think I'm dead,
but that will not concern me.

Some poet said galaxies
are a good place to hide—in a thicket of stars.
But any Kentucky thicket would be good enough for me;
there I could secretly watch small creatures
who want to go hide. And then I'll know
the thousand and one ways to be
and to be unknown.

It might seem like playing God on a small scale.
But God doesn't mind. God likes to pretend
at being God on a small scale.

What is an Anti-Poem?

How could I ever write an anti-poem? If I did, I would not know it, would hardly notice anything had been written. I would not care to read it myself or even acknowledge it as my own. Booted out of the door, it would wander forlornly, looking for a home in any poor anthology, or a magazine or even just a college print-off—one that seems to favor anti-style, but really doesn't because it is too concerned with setting a style.

This little litter of anti-words would be something you picked up on the street, or photographed like graffiti on an alley wall with the words chopped at the edges. No, this poem is not *anti* anything, doesn't rant and rage, or pick a fight, or politely schmooze with any society, high or low. It drifts off into a wasteland of things half said, follows no intention, and half wonders what it meant to say. Its only comfort is to lie down in a heap of silence and forget anything was said at all.

I will never hear of what became of this anti-poem and would hardly remember it. At best, in a moment of silence there might be an inkling of a nameless something that is happy it no longer is, because it scarcely had been, and the world is just as well without it.

No use making a definition of an anti-poem, since it never had any definition.

The Grammar of Be/cause

Mom would answer "because . . ."
when I asked "why can't I?"

"because" . . . left as a dangling conjunctive.

Be/cause, a categorical imperative:
a moral principle sufficient unto itself
in the realm of causes.

Because answers directly to "why?"

> Because.
> Because why?
> Because . . .

> But why?

Because I'm your Mother, that's why—
        collapsing *because* in-
to that womb of ultimate causality.

"*Because*": cryptic unto the point of obviousness
        a common-sense commonplace

intrinsic self-evidence
entitled to be unto
ultimate cause of be/causes.

That Barbarian in the Mirror

How thoughtlessly I raise my chin every morning
and set razor to my barbed neck, and there, face to face with myself,
enact a casual rite of suicide. It frightens me not the least
and proves in fact I'm willing to go on living, yes
until this time tomorrow. Then I will repeat
the old mindless masque of victim and executor, lift blade to neck
in unbloody sacrifice to tidy me up for the treacherous world.

I don't believe in my own sad ritual and have forgotten its meaning.
I do it the same as Dad, who twisted the Gillette and lifted
a thin razor to his jugular vein, not quite as his father did when
     religion was real,
handling lethal, straight blades and strop. Such vestiges of bloody sacrifice
were doomed by electric shavers.

Meanwhile reports of suicide are on the rise
since no daily ceremony raises awareness
against a civilized man's savage slasher—
the barbarian in the mirror.

Emily, your spare lines

scarcely defined
emerged from blank
to blank to fade
a trace of persistent guesses—

whatever have you been?

Merton's anniversary

"passed" 50 years ago, they say.
Well, that number counts for nothing.
Better to say, "*subsists* in the ever untimed."

Years count not, no measure there is
for boundless embrace of All-time.
Was—is—will be
co-exist there
simultaneously.

Outside this, nothing is.
Time inside this revolves;
history is a closed circle
ever completed, ever changing.

Wearily we count out years
until counting proves of no account,
hours never diminished but grown full in
All-time.

We age in parcels—leave this behind,
gain that awhile, run headlong to bump into already;
smell afar the scent of beyond,
staying in nothing but the unstayed.

All-time is being
altogether.

A revolving disk with no outer rim,
whose center is everywhere.

Critical Change for Whom?

I take occasion to visit Fr. Matthew's room.
His mood is serious, troubled
with questions about the reality of things,
of this world. All that's at hand
he sweeps off—illusion. Reality is other, he says.
He's in serious condition, I think, in for critical change.

Being shy of such engagement,
I withhold—resist argument,
all except to say my preference
is to simplify, not complicate,
take what I see for what it is—
table here, bed there—
trust my mind is
anchored in the real.

I step from Matthew's room,
leave him to his dark concerns—

suddenly I wake, startled to find myself
elsewhere, alone, on a mattress prone,
under Orion, stars and night—

no table, no room, no Matthew,

already three years passed,
all except for this—the dream he knew
was a dream.

I'm glad I was wrong about that.

Orion drifts above, knocked akimbo.

Ground of Searching

I dreamt I was far
from home, wandering around
seeking for bedding.

All the mind's searching
is some such form of dozing—
this thought included.

Why such restless quests,
when, already at rest, I'm
wandering through God?

Last Conversation with Matthew

Awakened from sleep,
he told me, between throat rattles
he was dreaming of Admiral Byrd,
(I thought he said Admirable Bird)

"He lived in the Antarctic, was a recluse,
his health was poor and his house leaked.
He often visits me in my dreams.
He was a good man."

His gasping mouth held my eyes.
When I pulled away to see his eyes
they were looking into mine as
through a veil, very pale, weighted
under sagging lids, their blue
almost gone—a distant look,
as withdrawing to exploration
and the South Pole.

"I want a sip of . . . can't remember,
it's called—a green something . . ."
We brought a can of Sprite.

(I think he meant Spirit.)

For Fr. Matthew Kelty

Uprooted oak left
shallow crater remaining
after many years.

This kind man, long dead,
stays nonetheless—still missed in
slopes of memory.

Our feet unheeding
drop clumsily down and up
grassy, shadeless dip

treading unseen pit
of that monumental past—
cool shade lingering.

Teensy, Weensy Fishies

As tiny as that, she said,
pinching fingers close to her eyes,
peered through the gap,
and said you once no bigger were
than that.

(Just a big sister tale,
I thought.)

You were in fact,
when you began,
teensy, eensy, weensy fishies.

I didn't believe a word.
What kind of story was that?

Sincere she was, confusing—
like as if Dad went fishing,
caught us, and it had nothing to do with Mom?

She added Fairytale to Fable
saying the stream was inside Daddy.
Now at this I could no longer . . .

What Mom had said alone seemed clear:
From God you came;
the rest perplexing all and queer.

Unto this day so it remains.
Explanations with *whats* and *hows*,
all incidental that can't surpass
what Mother said plain and clear:
from God it was you came.

Hidden Life

I just want to go hide. They'll all think I'm dead,
but that will not concern me. One poet said galaxies
are a good place to hide in a thicket of stars.
But a Kentucky thicket would be good enough for me;
there I could secretly watch other creatures
who want to go hide. And then I'll know
the thousand and one ways to be
and to be unknown.

It will seem like playing God on a small scale.
But God doesn't mind. God likes to pretend
at being God on a small scale.

II
Busy at Non-Doing

For Br. Martin de Porres

Set on slow simmer
months and years
flavors releasing
a touch of sage
given a watching
a sleep
a watching more

a glance at
the ground
at a slope
how it shifted
remembered
down
from where it was

down the slump
in the weary chair
light weighs from
the window
down

bending the head,
bending the gaze
to the simmer

the slow reduced
simmering of
a sage

A Song

The ground, the ground,
the ground only,
and more, the ground.

I put down another book
and gaze out the window
and think I might possibly finish it.

The ground, the ground,
only the ground,
and more, the ground.

My laundry folded,
not tired enough to nap,
I wonder at the mute-gray surround

The ground, the ground,
Ah the ground,
and more, the ground.

I take a chair and sink
into a pool of lamplight,
and sink into light, into light.

The ground, the ground,
ever the ground,
and more, the ground.

Was there only one second
I missed? Or such
continuity as

the ground, the ground,
the gray-wet ground
and only the ground.

What slips between the in
and the out of my breath?
What does the mountain
always know?

The ground, the ground,
the ground only,
and more, the ground.

Ode to Prime Matter
by Aristotle

Hail Holy Matter,
Matrix of change,
silent music of swift and slow,
unrocked cradle of time,
shapeless womb of space!

Seducing order
into scrawling form
across your blank playing-field,
enticing number,
teasing measure.

O Tabula Rasa,
unable to read, you are the blank slate,
scroll unwinding for the limitless Word.

Never positioned,
everywhere discovered,
unweighed in mass, in energy unmeasured,
in direction—trackless,
in position—indeterminate.

O fertile chaos, numb, mute, blind,
ignorant of what has been,
unconcerned for what is,
heedless of what might be,
devoid of regret for what cannot be.

O Materia Prima,
imprinted with vanishing ink.
O Prima Donna of scores unsung,
silent downbeat of Beethoven's Ninth,
breath inhaled to release Canticle of the Sun.

Prime Matter of everything that matters,
untouchable ground for everything firm.
O Mater Matter, endless potential
ever impending of God's concluding Amen.

Until the Next Committee

. . . unless there is need for further discussion
the matter should rest,
unless the issue be that if left to rest
it would raise the question as to whether the matter
matters,
with further questions about its meaning
and whether if left to rest
risks the innate tendency of matter
to remain inert matter and never
raise as an issue at all.

Kitchen utensils

... have a life of their own
every kitchen tool—it's not there when you want it
though you'd just put it down

... shows up after you grabbed
something else, sits there now to get in the way.

Sometimes one is gone for days—
no search can locate.
Then reappears—back from a vacation,

then lies around as if nothing happened.

After dish washing you put them up
like you have to put up with them,
or dump them in the drawers a-tumble,
a common grave so deep
you later can't find the thing urgently needed.

Knives can take a serious dislike to a particular cook,
slice off a fingertip—just like that!
And later without warning do it again—
the same finger!

Then there's the dirty skillet
that appears in the sink overnight,
left there to sleep after its wanton abandonment,
waiting for absolution.

Potholders just walk off, later found
heaped up, lazing together in an orgy.

There is the difficult spaghetti fork,
a shudder to see,
with long witchcraft tines made to torture.
In a panic you search for it
as the pasta is cooking past al dente.

Without cooks, O, what would they be,
those quirky, elusive things?
They'd have no busy hand to evade,
steal away or deceive. They would sink
into oblivion, forgetting they once
were more than steel and plastic,
alas, to stay put until the end of time.

The Fine Art of Frying an Egg

I counseled my mind with Renaissance Masters
of egg tempura and dreamt of an egg
fit for a Renaissance princess;

coddled an egg in a warmer,
through dark Vigils hour,
broke it out, egg white pre-whitened.

Then set it on low flame
of Faustus blue, subdued gas
of underworld magic reserved in darkness to rise,
ignite soundless, and delicately fry one exquisite egg

fit for Vermeer's young woman,
wearing a pearl earring.

Hungry ghosts

apparently visit the kitchen by night.

You find a few scoops of creamed corn gone,
> a swatch in the pan with the ladle left in.

A dozen beef patties at evening
> are only eight in the morning.
> cellophane cover lifted and left that way,
> or lid askew.

Bad children, not minding their manners,
> become hungry ghosts that way.

In the Eastern world they are everywhere, but
> They prefer only monasteries in the West.
> We all have some.

Wash your soup pot, darling—
> but no, it lands in the sink, spoon and all.

The time was we would blame a certain someone—
> Columban is feeding racoons.
> With Columban gone it continues.

> Thaddeus is gorging at night, he's so fat—
> but Thaddeus died and it still goes on.

> Ambrose is taking food to the poor—
> but unless he does that already dead and gone to heaven . . .

It is hungry ghosts, no doubt.

Who else would want cold creamed corn at night?

It's there

we say
of soup
seasoned
to a finish

So too a dying monk
fit for
the serving is
there

smacks true
of the salt
of being

when he's
there

tree
trunk
shadows

trundle
long
down
lawn

Equi
nox
sun
slung
low
casts
heavy
shade
cords

light
sung
such
bright
chords

stopped my
heart
half a
beat

shook
spirit
free

to pass
o
ver
to
another

sweeter
solar
cycle

Cedar Sails

How cedars love winds
sweeping bough sails while they stand
fixed, going nowhere!

Winds spreading strange tales
of choice trees who went abroad,
as wood for sea ships—

severed from their roots.

Nine-Tailed Tiger

Thunder spoke in long
grand sentences that stretched to
distant horizons—

thunder truck lumbered
over rocky clouds hauling
loosely stacked lumber,

plywood picked up from
tornado-demolished homes
in Louisiana.

No one argues with
Force of Nature. It strides by
without excuses.

Only afterward
we view dire consequences
for good or for ill.

Three days getting here,
winds slowed down to benign,
mute placidity.

That tornado of
nine tails has drifted asleep,
soft, warm pussy cat.

Meanwhiles

. . . that is—all of life
between my birth and death.

No, not always mean.
Yes, it does mean, and stands as
the golden mean between
waxing and waning.

Meanwhile the serene moon wiles away its
time in the heavens,

while I step smart to get to Terce
with chagrin at my ever chasing down time
to catch up, to save, to spend,
squander or consume
until full of meanwhiles
I drop to a halt consumed by

time in its idle wiles
and my harried meanwhiles are all
borne off upon oblivion.

III
A Community of Creatures

Gang Crows

Crows having a blast,
they're the only clowns in town
these dreary, cold days.

Winter's silence got
gobbled up and spit out with
broadcast sound bites.

Raw, raucous show, they're
flinging sassy sarcasms
at staid, pompous skies.

Noble Bugs

Insects love to die
slammed flat inside book pages.
Often do I find

moth positioned well,
pressed like blossom preserved of
Victorian lass.

Carelessly I'd shut
one flecked fly smudged a-kimbo,
marking words inspired—

black asterisk fixed
next *tragedy, desire,* or
immortality.

A Little Night Music

Cortle-twurtle sounds
from moonlit valley, young coon
gone out moonlighting.

Across frosted field
returns reply—let's make songs
of raccoon desire.

Low, in dark grass, lone
cricket plays tiny fiddle—
sweet twit-turewl rhymes.

Moon fades. Bridegroom sun
peeping up, gazes warmly
on fair, pale-faced moon.

Scent of Winter

Wilted grass is grown green again
from lingering rainfall.
Scents rise darkened by moldering leaves,
mingling with memories of April;
rich, brief brew of odors—careless
of oncoming snow.

Soft spray hangs heavy in air,
pale gauze, down to dimmed horizons;
quiet country secluded,
sunken in dense sleep.

A lull in time has blurred all of
WAS and SHALL BE. Time rests
in seamless dreams of IS.

Through such thick scents I step slowly,
scarcely sensing what drift
of dim longings are therein concealed.

Sole Calet in Hieme
Peter Abelard (1079–1142)

Sun in winter warms
a pauper needing fire.
For charm of nightly lamps
the pauper has moon and stars.

No rich man's ivory divan—
on hay the poor reclines.
There birds pluck out thrilling songs,
fragrant flowers waft abroad.

At great expense the wealthy
construct a house that crumbles,
depicted with phony sun of sorts,
fake stars like those above.

Inside the vault of heaven's chamber
the pauper in splendor reclines.
A real sun there, with actual stars
the Lord himself depicted.

Solstice Eclipse

My eyes awaken to silence,
silence enfolded in snow,
snow seeping to snowmelt,
melting in ground sleeping through solstice,
a solstice shadowing silence.

Swollen full, the moon
slips into earth's shadow,
darkens behind clouds
that curtain my steady gaze
upon dimming moon's
slow, steady submission to silence.

Winter Night Symposium

Quarter moon converses with clouds
in lofty symposium—casual, musing, floating
ideas, adrift in thought, passing off bons mots,
with subtle nuance, obscure allusions,
something elliptic, something recondite,
something of hope.

Cryptic remarks emerge and ride
in open delight, hints of dreams
lingering on, lightly veiled,
semi-tone threads of
secret aspirations.

Swift memories arise,
tumble headlong in shades of amber, blue, and gray;
gather, glare, and fade when a buzzard cloud sails in,
blacks out just long enough to say:
even this will pass.

So onward goes the discourse,
with subtlety, brilliance,
gentle wit—ever the matchless woman holds sway
in timeless symposium of dear, familiar,
ever nimble clouds.

Juncos Came Back

Quick dark specks
Fly random zips
Canvass wide court
Check broad stretch,

Criss-cross yard,
Twit and Pip:
Keenly curious
"Hey, let's stay."

Hard winter comes.
Dour King Cold,
Bright Queen Snow,
Hold royal court.

Sturdy juncos,
Greyfriar jesters,
Play merrily on
All season long.

Cedar Sails

Oh, cedars love winds
sweeping their sails, while they stand,
stayed, going nowhere!

Winds speaking strange tales
of trees gone far abroad on
seas as wooden ships.

Trees lost of roots in service.

Frost Edges

Frost forms on edges of things,
hedges and eaves, on railings and trees,
in sunlit grass lavish diamonds
scattered abroad,
while heat pours on
to steal them away
right there
in broad daylight,

a masterful thief.

Polar Bear

The polar bear

has a certain way

of being in the world

which is not

for everyone to know about

or anybody, anyway

not a polar bear

who knows it

by being in the world

just that way

a polar bear.

Winter Conversation of Trees

Bare elm sustains posture
of personal uplift.

Spruce retains widow's garb
for propriety's sake.

Complex cherry branches look cross.

Tearless weeping willow
faints earthward
from summer's heavy losses.

Cottonwood widely embraces year's completion.

Gingko finely probes every minute detail of space.

Cedar of Lebanon—straightforward
in all he speaks or tells.

All herewith written
is foreign language unto
their lofty discourse.

Rain Mass

Enormous choir in
monotone *Ordinary*
of rain poured down

massive chant. Sacred Mass

soon slacked off in soft
diminuendo, soaking into
mute, sated grass.

Rothko Sky

Dark clouds adrift with
faint, shy gradations of gray,
dim implications of night.

Immense Rothko chap-
el, devoid of design, cre-a-
tion—yet unbegun.

Parental Winds

Winds, with long range plans,
sound them out in trees—in rounds
pausing, resuming,

with muffled voices—
our parents talking things out
with kids put to bed

going over it
again, louder, softer now,
low tone, light reply,

comforting murmurs,
looking after kids' concerns
on new weather front.

Groaning snow

under my boot
wants to know
who are you?

Kitty-cat tracks
tell a pretty tale,
such delicate trace
whispers of grace.

Traveling Companion

Low winter sun
bars with shadows
the tree lined road.
Only specters travel here.
But these bold boots of mine
claim ready passage.

My warm companion seems
to keep apace with every step,
strolls atop the far slope.
My unspoken thoughts
he must conjecture, yet
offers no reply.
His steady look
I cannot read, too bright his face,
though nothing there be hidden.

He silently admits to
evening's swift advance,
as shadows creep upward
and floods of cold rise higher.

Warmth lifts and westward drifts
with that grand traveler
swiftly departing with
                    long ranging stride.

Mild January Eve

Slow wind gently shifts
Spruce boughs—some unheard music
only spruce trees hear.

Afternoon shadows slant
across damp asphalt, blue
sky glancing off puddles.

In this world of chance
where much goes wrong, how whole, how
one this pause in time,

this shifting hour
when contentment fills dark spruces,
waiting for sunset.

Wealthy Abandon

Abundant peonies
tumble over garden wall
drunken on night air,

shed lacy litter,
frail, white filaments, tears of
young, abandoned love.

Swelling pods remain,
memory fills, hoping to
burst on better days.

Fantasy House Plants

You bougainvillea,
perfect monster of a plant
reaching out tendrils

cracking dry seed pods!
You'd take over the world
given half a chance.

Flowers redeem you.

You bristling aloe
green blades threaten every side,
screaming don't touch me!

When broken, life oozes out,
milky mercy for scorched skin—
kind nurse with a mean face.

Orchids forming buds,
string out Japanese lanterns
preparing to shine
on green leaf couches
where sprites and fairies come to
luxuriate with

gods thriving on air.

Little Mt. Rushmore, KY

Found at the back end of monks' grounds.
Limestone carved by water and time displays
one wrinkle-browed President
     with pouty under lip,
one pinched face President, bitter,
     with no nose for politics or anything else,
one recondite sage who has seen it all
     and knows better than to tell;

one fat, tiny, upstart dwarf
     all ready to promote iniquity;
one dent-mouth Indian chief
     damaged by old memories
too deep to bear.

All hidden away under an evergreen cove.
No public access.

Pastel Blossoms

Blossoms on tulip trees
not true tulips be,
only tulip wannabes

I climbed aloft
peered into pastel cup
found its face painted up
with delicate sunrise—

inside its shy, meek heart
gentle firework splays,
delicate displays for grandmas, saints
and smiling maids

or old tree-top boys
having a lark.

Careful Instruction

In declarative
sentences, Robin explains
true order of things.

By sunrise this will
have been quite comprehensive:
Summa Omnibus.

Every harmony,
each discord nicely outlined
in careful sequence.

But where are students?
Who? Unless the air, the tree
and I care to hear.

Attention Getter

Summer mockingbird
shouts entertainment to point
of annoyance, yes

he's got too many
ideas. Puts it all out there
in long, mad tumble.

During winter, his dry, sharp
twack-twack is sheer annoyance.
Sociable—but crude.

Got to love him anyway.

Jail Girls

I sit still long enough
to see through a tree
Venus and Moon jailed
inside same cage of branches.
Two vagrant girls,
uncomfortable strangers
held on suspicion,
set apart on separate sides.

Come dawn, they sailed forth together,
by trials of a night made
angels on a lark.

Next night saw the pair—
Venus forging ahead,
Moon smudged, waning thin
slowly falling back—
big girl can't keep up with
sweet pearl of the sky.

They'll go separate ways,
and meet in a month or two
for another late-night fling.

Cresting Green

Cloud-smudged sun, orange-red,
lifts beyond checker-patch clouds.
Lone locust sounds pitch.

Grass crowds with dense rage,
wild, lush, pushing high in fields;
trees—surging green waves,

surf tide returning,
subsiding slowly year by
year, splashing green waves

suspended, in air
crest, drain off, leaving bare trunks—
masts anchored in port.

Summer surging greens,
winter ebbing grays—what are trees,
but waves, ceaseless waves.

Rowdy Party

Great hilarity—
coyote laughing it up,
loud, late, wild party,
revved up to shrill pitch,
quivering fiddles, coyotes
really cutting loose.

Strong reproaches from
neighborhood dog yells complaints:
Hey! I need some sleep!
Well, we can be sure,
weather permitting, they'll be
at it tomorrow.

Great Art

Approaching rain
applauds like millennia,
then passes and fades.
Ages remember
great art, but ages likewise
forget and depart.

Rasping of locusts
remains—it's their daily task.
Slow, small drops of hope
drip into silence
where here is no more than here:
now is all that's now.

Light startled my page
when rain clouds opened up white—
thund'rous mountain clouds—
Is art ready for
this?   Huff, Huff! Hidden deer spoke
spying from forest:

"Even this must pass."

Spider

Anni nostri sicut aranea meditabitur . . .
Psalm 89:10

has lost her honorable mention in the Psalms,
lost since Greek and Latin Bible days:
    Our years like a spider's are to be pondered . . .

Thus was Scripture's single bow
to that round, ponderous brain of Aranea,
that fertile cranium, that active abdomen
whence long, fine threads of thought spun out,
daily meditations sewn in superb order,
intricate designs, conceptual connections,
subtle genius of geometrical air,
poised to catch, comprehend, and grasp
its small world's living contingencies!

Poised motionless, suspended in meditation,
she, with still, slow, bated breath,
senses sudden pluck sounded on outspread strings.
Out she speeds to a bug in distress
to wrap, package, and ponder it
for weeks on end.

Days later her philosophy is found in shreds.
The torn web is vacant. It was a strange
and awesome strife when thought and Reality
contended—conceptual lassos skillfully flung,
ideas spun to apprehend, stick,
and wrap snug a wasp within comprehension.

But Reality fiercely buzzed, stung
and carried off her full mind limp,
alive and numbed to the Victor's nursery.
A mud-daubed tunnel now holds her Gray Eminence
tucked away with hungry larvae.

Consumed in time, she'll be transformed to something
other;
. . . for none can see God and live.

Alas, Scripture's Sacred Memorial to Aranea
is erased and all we now read is:

> *Our life is over like a sigh . . .*

Ever'bubby's Mum

Just like Pentecost—
Mockingbird sings in strange tongues
He's done seen Jesus!

Much talkety-talk
from high pulpit—Mockingbird
just goes on and on.

All night lullabies
keep poor sleepers awake
—ever'bubby's Mum.

Just like Pentecost—
Mockingbird sings out strange tongues:
He's done seen Jesus!

The Heavens Expound

Faint, distant thunder
carries ancient narration
along horizons.

Forest front trembles,
old storm rumors meet hard facts,
raining on leaf ears.

Sky splits with raw truth,
pronouncement hurled end to end
releasing deluge.

I dance in its cleansing
while judgment pounds like thunder
to kick me to life,

laughing loud at how
terror scuttled me to porch—
What's with that old kid!

With all that, did he learn what?

Fireflies

What do they seek for?
flying with body lamps all night—
on-off—resting not,

searching out darkness—
off-on, capturing no night
hard as they could try,

seeing only when
trying ceases. Then night crowds in.
Dark flees lamps lifted,

cautiously hides from
that fly-filled field spread with
lonely, drifting stars

that never collide—
earthly constellations swarming
the dark, grassy range

ever without owning it.

Hay Roll Calving

Hay roll tractor
totters round the slope,
slow as an old farmer in a hat,
leaning on the setting sun,
turning slowly to follow
long dry trails of raked hay.

It scarfs it up,
leaves the field clean,
digesting until slowed to
a thoughtful pause,
lifts its tail hood,
and calves the roll
onto the ground
with great relief.

Then indifferent, turns away
onto another row,
circling the field
to get progeny more.

Comes morning,
a scattered herd
of perfect, round bales
are populating the hill,
sculptures of a mind
that sees the world is round.
And the rising sun too,
with round face, smiles.

Ripe Madonna

Deep, green magnolia
sways heavily in south wind
gently lifting skirts.

Laden with red pods,
Nobilissima Donna
tosses head to tunes,

rolls broad, heavy hips
with laughter at southern breeze—
such balmy love songs!

How ripe her age for dancing!

Sound Unsounded

Sunrise sustained bright
sound—unsounded.

From mid-air rooster snatched
pitch—high suspended there,
released it back to unheard
scales of sunrise.

Careful call of dove ascends,
sounds aspiration, then fails—
fails in soft, descending plaints.

One Pee-Wee puts it precisely—
"shy notes need be petite."

Abrupt tower bell nails it—
nails it steady,
in relentless
strokes. I rise—
rise for Tierce
and leave morning free,
to sheer, bright,

unsounded sound.

Thunder Disputes

Commotion in sky
here and about—remainder
of thunder disputes.

Long, glum lull ensued.
Sky fills, hot flashes flare up;
slow rain settles in.

It'll take all day
of sullen rain to forget—
put it all behind.

Meanwhile passing geese
laugh it off, which once more sets
the thunder complaining.

Wishing Trees

Along the windy trail
wishing trees whisper at skies
their secret, lofty wishes
with ceaseless, breathy sighs.

Heady wind onward pressed
could scarcely bear to hear
wishes caught in branches
ignored from year to year.

Autumn Evening

End of Compline daily marks
our Grand Silence, night's retirement.
I step out, passing the sun, feeling grass underfoot,
treading shoeless to a hideaway.

These day-deafened ears open upon exquisite silence,
entranced by dry thrash of leaves kicked,
lulled by faint barks from distant woods.

The sun finds earlier repose each evening.
Twilight shades mute the contours
of fields and hills.
Orange light suffuses the sky,
dimming away into deeper blue.

A single star, Vega, stands.
Stands the silver moon.

Birds are silent, crickets stilled.
Summer, reclining for slumber,
slips into dreams of autumn.

IV
Ritual Instinct

Hollow Bell

Compline bell sounds hollow
in the early nightfall
tired of the day and
contented with dark

Gather your garments about you
little beast, the cold will not
swallow you up. Hide in
the quiet and curl up in the night.

A little mingling of song.
A candle for a boy.
A candle for a mother.

November Sesshin

To sit with others
in silence—to forget them
in awareness that

every awareness
is one. To hear the same crows
the tattle of leaves

blowing a-scuttle,
the far hum of hay mower—
the unsounding sun

penetrates us deep—
Meister of Awareness,
first of all saints—light.

Fourth Sunday in Advent

At Merton's hermitage

Election results in, I come,
take refuge out of the way,
out of noise, outdoor sanctuary.

Damp, lazy leaves limp
along matted ground; stall, halt,
and flip at wind reversals.

Wind-chime spoke one faint ding
at tall rooted Cross on which
one wagon wheel leans and waits.

A stand of bare scrub trees,
forgetting autumn, holds congested station,
patient upon a platform of leaves

under swift, dense canopy of clouds,
waits as commuters northbound,
urgent with imponderable change.

A Musical Riddle

The kind of instrument I make music with
ranks as the finest among music makers.
It is both reed and string. It's most subtle in nuance,
most flexible in pitch, unique in tone for each user,
improving its tone with regular practice.
It suits the age of every player and always fits her size.
No one can purchase it, much be spent in learning it,
much gained in using it, while using it not diminishes life.

No other instrument is designed by God,
none so tooled for immanent rapture,
none so bound to the human heart. Without the heart
it dries up and shrivels, with the heart
it expands and thrills.

With one such instrument, to be lost when I am gone,
my life has been a song, and I'll always sing to live.

Reading the Clouds

After too much time reading Hebrew
a stone-gray tablet-cloud bears a worn texture
of ancient lettering, vowels, and consonants
all waiting separately, speckly gamets and segols here,
weedy shins, vavs and lameds there,
ready to be assembled into final revelations,
once the world finally finds its meaning

later today, perhaps.

Patron Saint of Music

Cecilia sings one note
eternally sustained,
containing undertones/overtones
the total range past hearing,
sum and summary, full
pleroma of harmony.

One simple beat for rhythm,
one long gravity wave stretched
from time's beginning to end,
pedal point for circling spheres.

Pitch precisely set to key
unlocking music's treasury
hid within the yawning vault
of silence all encompassing.

The ancient mode set to tonic note
rarefying every modal tone
with inebriating tonic
wafted up on singing ayre.

Her scale stretched from earth to heaven
where angels downward run
and up silver rungs sustained
by one subtle ring. Cecilia
sings throughout eternity.

In the morning I come before you

watching and waiting

watching

then

waiting

waiting

and

watching

tired of watching

I wait.

When I waited

enough

I watch.

When watch and wait

are not enough

I disregard enough

for You are

enough.

When You are

enough

I am
enough

when I am

enough

You are

enough

enough

that You are

watching

and waiting

and my

watching and waiting

is Your

watching and waiting.

Bells Embossed with Names

St. Thomas bell in key of E
doubtfully calls
     for
Evidence
Evidence.

Raphael bell in key of G
paws on sheltering clouds
in muted tones
Gee! . . . Gee!
pets soft humid air
Gee! Gee!

St. Mary bell in tones of C
Warmly sounds
Consolation
Consolation.

Ringing together
the rollicking three
occasion loud festivity
tumble down hilarity
 of angels
  from sky
   to ground.

Portrait of Rilke

whose young, devouring eyes
were broken by the Great War;

eyes caught in caged leopard's eyes,
pacing bars in desperate spin,
poet now an image trapped within,
shuddering down rippling limbs
to finish in the end;

Eyes whose upward glance swung
to the Great Rose Window,
spun down that Tiger's vast
devouring eye, swirled in whirlpool beyond limit;

. . . whose open eyes plunged through every
splintered shard of death
  and burst into

the Open.

Noel Drizzle

Faint drumming on eaves—
soft fingertips of rain for
newborn Jesus child.

Thrumming suspended,
silence fell, for babe in barn
must sleep awhile.

Taps of random drops
mark time till pale dawn tiptoes
to waken boy child

Epiphany Gifts

Enough for this child—
frost sparkling diamond bright
when Magi brought gold.

Enough for this man—
sunlit water poured glistening
from lifted conch shell.

Enough for this son—
warm glow on mother's proud face
at water turned wine.

Walking Meditation

I drift barefooted in dew-drenched grass
wandering a crop of crosses
where monks proceeding me
await my reception

outside of time.

I sense a kind acquaintance
at each step pressed in grass
soles to souls
assembled below

outside of space.

The wash of dew is cleansing,
is peace, and pleasure.
This brief moment awaits
that blink of eternity's
eye encompassing

time and space.

ABOUT PARACLETE PRESS

Who We Are

As the publishing arm of the Community of Jesus, Paraclete Press presents a full expression of Christian belief and practice—from Catholic to Evangelical, from Protestant to Orthodox, reflecting the ecumenical charism of the Community and its dedication to sacred music, the fine arts, and the written word. We publish books, recordings, sheet music, and video/DVDs that nourish the vibrant life of the church and its people.

What We Are Doing

BOOKS | PARACLETE PRESS BOOKS show the richness and depth of what it means to be Christian. While Benedictine spirituality is at the heart of who we are and all that we do, our books reflect the Christian experience across many cultures, time periods, and houses of worship.

We have many series, including *Paraclete Essentials*; *Paraclete Fiction*; *Paraclete Poetry*; *Paraclete Giants*; and for children and adults, *All God's Creatures*, books about animals and faith; and *San Damiano Books*, focusing on Franciscan spirituality. Others include *Voices from the Monastery* (men and women monastics writing about living a spiritual life today), *Active Prayer*, and new for young readers: *The Pope's Cat*. We also specialize in gift books for children on the occasions of Baptism and First Communion, as well as other important times in a child's life, and books that bring creativity and liveliness to any adult spiritual life.

The MOUNT TABOR BOOKS series focuses on the arts and literature as well as liturgical worship and spirituality; it was created in conjunction with the Mount Tabor Ecumenical Centre for Art and Spirituality in Barga, Italy.

MUSIC | The PARACLETE RECORDINGS label represents the internationally acclaimed choir *Gloriæ Dei Cantores*, the *Gloriæ Dei Cantores Schola*, and the other instrumental artists of the *Arts Empowering Life Foundation*.

Paraclete Press is the exclusive North American distributor for the Gregorian chant recordings from St. Peter's Abbey in Solesmes, France. Paraclete also carries all of the Solesmes chant publications for Mass and the Divine Office, as well as their academic research publications.

In addition, PARACLETE PRESS SHEET MUSIC publishes the work of today's finest composers of sacred choral music, annually reviewing over 1,000 works and releasing between 40 and 60 works for both choir and organ.

VIDEO | Our video/DVDs offer spiritual help, healing, and biblical guidance for a broad range of life issues including grief and loss, marriage, forgiveness, facing death, understanding suicide, bullying, addictions, Alzheimer's, and Christian formation.

Learn more about us at our website:
www.paracletepress.com
or phone us toll-free at 1.800.451.5006

SCAN
TO
READ
MORE